To: Lennon &
James, you can FIND
Hope you can FIND
a crow for a friend)
A crow for a friend.

Samuka Butcon
2016

SYD,

The Crow

**Based on a True Story
of a Wild Crow Who
Befriended Two Kids**

by

**Lenore Kay, Jason Janetzke
and Linda Bolton**

Illustrations by Sheila McLaughlin

Syd, The Crow©™

Copyright Protections

Syd, The Crow©™

Summary and Acknowledgements

It's almost impossible for humans to develop a friendship with a wild animal. But, the opposite can happen. This story is about a wild crow that consciously picked a family and developed a relationship with humans…and a dog.

Based on a true story, this book is almost 40 years in the making. Like a contemporary version of *Mary Had a Little Lamb*, Syd, the crow, became a family friend and followed the kids to school one day. This close encounter of a third kind with a wild crow -- forever changed our understanding of animal behavior. In retrospect, we now realize how rare this experience was. Researching more about crows has unearthed a plethora of information on crow intelligence. Both admired and vilified, like the Yin and Yang of life itself, crows have intrigued and fascinated people worldwide and have worked their way into cultures, art, music and literature. Keen observers have taken note of the crow's unique language, their use of tools which was thought to be the defining characteristic exclusive to humans, and their most amazing capability -- the crow's ability to recognize individual human faces in a crowd.

Not knowing any of this, our family witnessed all these talents firsthand and can now share our story with the world. Our memories are like sparkling shimmers on the water, and we have many to thank.

Ms. Sheila McLaughlin, the illustrious illustrator, who not only drew pictures as though she was in the room as an eye witness –- but also provided valuable input, adding richness and texture to old photos and verbal images.

Mr. Dave Bazinet, the computer guru and artistic director, for his painstaking designs and enhancements.

Ms. Judy Smith, the professional editor, for her guidance and close attention to detail.

Mr. Michael McPherrin, the former principal of Roosevelt School who confirmed his memories of the crow encounter, added more detail and allowed us to use his name and image.

Ms. Patti Fuchs, the Director of the Children's Deptartment at Indian River County Library, Vero Beach, Florida, for her feedback and guidance identifying Syd, The Crow as a hybrid book - to read to a child – and for a child to read.

Ms. Carol Rynk, Assistant Librarian, Childrens Department, Spanish River Library, Boca Raton, Florida.

The current residents of the old house in Elmhurst, Illinois, who were kind enough to permit a visit.

The Family Grandsons:

Tommy Kay, age 13; for his point-by-point critique of the story, pictures, colors and fonts.

Alex Janetzke, age 10; for his endorsement of a great story from his father's childhood.

Max Janetzke, age 4; for sitting long enough to hear the story and not fall asleep.

The Family Members:

Ms. Lenore Kay, co-author, for her steadfast adherence to the truth of the story – allowing some poetic license.

Mr. Jason Janetzke, co-author, for his encouragement to start, finish and publish this story.

Mr. Dennis Janetzke, **Auntie Celeste Scheffler**, and all the cherished family members in the story.

This book is dedicated to places we'll remember all our lives, but now have changed. These special places have their moments with friends and family we love so well. Some are dead and some are living, but all live vividly in memories and stories that forever warm our hearts.

Paraphrased from the song "In My Life" by The Beatles.

We hope this book helps
to reveal the undiscovered
intelligence of animals.

I f we could capture the arrow of time,

we'd understand that we lived in an

enchanted moment...but didn't know it was

going to be so good, so real, and so fleeting.

I n the mid 1970's, the Janetzke family lived in an old

wood-frame house in Elmhurst, Illinois, a suburb of

Chicago. Elmhurst was named for its many tree-

lined streets that formed living arches of old elm trees.

T he neighborhood off York Road was full of children

and was a nice place to raise a family. Most of the time

we didn't even lock our doors, because we all looked

out for each other. Many houses had a special metal

box at the front door for the milkman. Every morning at 5 am, the milkman would

leave fresh milk in glass bottles, and everyday we'd leave money in the box to pay

him. The boxes were not locked. No one would ever think to take the money.

It was an honor system.

The house had an old-fashioned cistern that collected rainwater from the roof and stored it in a large underground tank. That water could then be pumped out to the yard to water the lawn and vegetable garden. Today, that's called water "re-use" and is considered very "green."

he front door of the screened-in porch had a letter slot the mailman would use to deliver the mail. The problem was that Pixie, the family pooch, was very territorial. Even though the mailman came every day, she never got used to him. Pixie was sure the mailman was an intruder. With an angry growl, she'd try to grab the mailman's hand through the small opening. Of course, she couldn't so she'd grab the mail instead as it came through the slot. The family letters and bills often came in full of holes and bite marks. When we heard all the commotion at the front door, we'd have to rush to stop her in her tug-of-war with the mailman, who didn't appreciate the excitement -- even though it was kind of funny.

Almost everyone in the family had some kind of musical talent. Grandpa Lenckos played the clarinet and saxophone. Uncle Eddie played the piano, while both Uncle Iggy and Uncle Leo played the violin. Because most of the family members had their birthdays around holidays, the entire extended family would gather at the Janetzke house on Mother's Day, Thanksgiving and Christmas.

After a big turkey dinner, we gathered in the large living room and had so much fun with live music, dancing and singing. Uncle Victor loved dancing with Little Lenore, especially to the traditional Polish Christmas Carols, called Kolendy.

There was a big yard that extended around the side of the house. Dad loved to work outside mowing the lawn and washing the cars. Mom loved to decorate and make the old house look prettier and prettier. They decorated the house so nicely that the local church asked the Janetzkes to open their house to the public for a "house-walk". People actually bought tickets to come and see the house with English wallpaper and new drapes mixed with a large round antique dining room table made of solid oak, and a tall grandfather's clock with beveled-edge glass panes. The old house felt like a warm, comfortable and happy home.

When our daughter Lenore was about 10 years old, she signed up for just about every school activity ever invented: violin, piano, recorder, orchestra, Blue Birds, gymnastics and Indian Princesses with the local YMCA.

Jason, Lenore's little brother, was about 5 years old at the time. He loved playing in the backyard with his sister and Pixie, swinging on the swing set, and riding his brand new fire-engine red Schwinn bike, which he helped pay for by doing chores around the house.

There

was a huge horse chestnut tree

in front of the house that blossomed like a giant bouquet of white

flowers every spring and turned bright red and golden in the fall.

One of most amazing things about that tree happened every year.

11

Almost like clockwork, on Halloween night, it would suddenly drop all its leaves in a carpet of fall colors. One of the best things about our house was that remarkable tree. It was a neighborhood landmark!

inters in the Midwest were windy and long. Through the cold season, people would look for any sign of spring to give them hope for better weather. When the giant forsythia bush in the front yard started to turn light green, and then yellow, the family knew it was the first sign of warmer days ahead.

om would always watch the children play in the back yard from the corner window in the kitchen. As they played and Dad worked outside – no one noticed a crow flying around the backyard observing the family. Early one summer day while Lenore and Jason were playing on the swing set, Mom noticed that a crow landed on the outside ledge of the corner kitchen window. She thought, "Wow! How cool is this?"

he crow was a very big bird with shiny black feathers that sparkled with iridescent purples and greens in the sunlight. It was just sitting there, looking into the kitchen, when Lenore tore up the back stairs and threw open the screen door shouting, "Mommy! Mommy! There's a crow outside our kitchen window!"

t first, the family didn't know what, if anything, the crow wanted. They thought maybe it was hurt or sick, but it kept flying around and seemed fine. Getting a little superstitious, they even wondered if it was a sign of things to come…maybe an omen. Then, to their surprise, the crow started bringing small gifts and leaving them on the window

sill. The family quickly realized this bird is communicating…it has personality!

om went out to get a better look when Dad said, "Maybe he's hungry. Let's feed him something." They tore up slices of bread and carefully lined them up on the outside windowsill. The family all watched silently, almost holding their breath, to see what the crow would do. Then all of a sudden Jason shouted, "Look, look, he's eating them!" Beaming with joy, Lenore said, "We've got a new pet! What should we call him?" No one remembers why but just then Dad suggested, "Syd" and that was the beginning of a wonderful adventure with this very special crow.

14

It wasn't long and Syd became part of the family. We would see him eat Pixie's food right out of her dog dish, but Pixie didn't mind, Syd was eating like a bird. Through the dining room window, we'd see him go to bed every night exactly at nine o'clock in the nest he had built in the big blue spruce tree at the side of the house. Syd hung out in our backyard from late summer until that next spring. We laughed when Syd brought a silver gum wrapper to the window and presented it like a gift. We all thought it his way of saying, "Thank you for the bread," or just a way to show off his favorite things.

e soon realized that Syd really liked shiny objects...anything that sparkled and caught the sunlight. He would present them, then take them to his nest or secret hiding place, because he'd show them to us...and then they'd be gone. Sometimes it was an old pop top from a soda bottle, another time it was a red, chunky plastic ring that Syd had 'stolen' from some child's sandbox. Mom commented that he's acting like the crow in the opera "The Thieving Magpie" which nearly cost the main character her life because the villagers thought she was stealing. He loved to show off how strong he was as he carried these treasures to us in his clawed talons.

yd had adopted us. He was out there all by himself in the backyard most of the time -- either soaring overhead with wings outstretched like feathery fingers and cawing or just sitting on the windowsill. We never saw any other crows. If we did, oddly enough, that would be called, "a murder of crows."

ne Saturday, Dad was outside washing the cars when Jason came up the driveway from a fast bike ride up and down the street. He sat on the back steps catching his breath when Syd suddenly swooped down to the pedals of his shiny red bike. The bicycle pedals were still spinning when Syd pecked and pecked at them to keep them turning. Jason called us over to see Syd's new trick. The crow was amusing himself by catching the sunlight in the reflective yellow strips on the spinning pedals.

yd was actually playing with us and our things…and maybe even thinking. We couldn't believe how involved the crow had become in our lives. This clever bird was providing a very special experience for our family.

t was wonderful!

fter a lazy summer playing joyfully with the neighborhood kids like Laurie, Ann, Matt and Pat, the leaves started changing color. It was time for Lenore and Jason to head back to school.

hey had to walk about four blocks west to the Roosevelt Elementary School on the corner of Grantley and Myrtle Avenues. On their way, they had to cross some side streets, but Lenore was old enough to look out for Jason and the other younger kids in the group.

enore was always a very responsible and protective big sister.

One day on their way to school, the children noticed a black crow flying overhead. Lenore shouted, "It looks like Syd!" The other kids asked, "Who's Syd?"

hen Lenore and Jason came home for lunch and saw Syd outside the kitchen window, they told Mom they thought he had followed them to school. Mom said, "Oh, that can't be! That's too far, and how would Syd know to look for just you two?"

ell, that very afternoon, Mom went to meet Lenore and Jason as they were coming home from school. The children were all excited and laughing like crazy. Syd had found Jason and was riding all the way home  ON TOP OF HIS HEAD! The other kids thought, "Wow! How cool is that to have a pet crow for a friend! Maybe he'll sit on my head. Maybe we can get one too!"

om couldn't believe her eyes. She saw Syd hitching a ride on top of Jason's head as she watched the kids coming down the street. When the group finally met up with Mom the children shouted, "Did you see that? Did you see Syd on Jason's head?" Mom was laughing so hard she could barely speak.

t was really happening!

**S**yd was just showing off!

**Y**elling and screaming kids

didn't scare him away.

**D**idn't he feel funny riding on Jason's head?

Syd was so brave to play with humans like that.

**he** family figured out that this magnificent black crow adored Lenore and Jason. Somehow, Syd was able to identify these two children from all the others –- and track their movements like a homing pigeon. But Mom and Dad worried because Syd was such a big distraction that the kids could be paying more attention to the bird than watching for cars on the street. Someone must have trained this crow. But, how do you control a very intelligent crow? What could they do?

**he** school principal told us later that he was concerned when he saw a large black crow swooping down from the trees, dive-bombing the children in the playground. The crow would land on a brick wall outside the kindergarten and caw at the kids. Syd must have been looking for Lenore and Jason but lost track of them when they entered the school building.

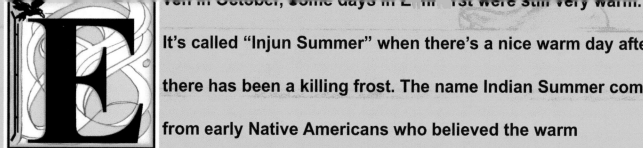

It's called "Injun Summer" when there's a nice warm day after there has been a killing frost. The name Indian Summer comes from early Native Americans who believed the warm

wind was sent by their southwestern god, Cautantowwit.[1]

t that time, most schools didn't have air conditioning. If the classroom got a little stuffy in the afternoon, the only relief was a cool breeze from an open window.

ne warm fall day, Lenore was in Miss Davis' fifth grade classroom on the second floor when the teacher opened the window for a little fresh air.

uddenly the students were distracted from their lessons: a crow started pecking at the wooden window sill, as if it wanted to attract someone's attention. Lenore saw it but didn't think too much about it because she immediately

recognized that it was "only Syd!"

iss Davis didn't know about a pet crow and probably wouldn't have believed Lenore if she said, "Don't worry! That's my pet crow, Syd." Some of the children were afraid because they thought the crow might attack them.

f course, Miss Davis had no idea what the crow was doing there. She thought, "We can't have a bird interfering with the class studies." As she went toward the window to close it, Syd made a dash into the classroom!

he crow flew around the room with Miss Davis trying to shoo it out with her blue sweater. She chased it while the children screamed with laughter at the silly sight.

ut no dice! Syd was having too much fun showing off for Lenore and her classmates. Frantic to gain control, the teacher sent a student to get the Principal. "Tell him to come up here right away. It's urgent! There's a wild bird in the room!"

r. McPherrin was the young, energetic Principal of Roosevelt Elementary and knew he had a problem on his hands when he saw what was going on in Miss Davis' room. The teacher was shouting to the children, "Be calm!" But the students were running around the room either trying to get away from the crow or trying to play with it. The crow was scared too, and was flapping his wings and cawing loudly as he tried to get away. All classroom rules and regulations were out the window, Lenore was shouting, "Don't hurt him! It's Syd! He's my pet!"

r. McPherrin had to take control. He said to the students: "Children, go back to your seats!" Then he and Miss Davis tried getting the crow back out the window. They formed a wall with their bodies and moved toward the window, but Syd wouldn't go. The crow was having too much fun chasing the children and did not understand that he was frightening some of them.

fter several attempts to get Syd out of the classroom, Mr. McPherrin was exhausted. He said, "Students, just ignore the crow and carry on as usual with your lessons!" Well, that didn't work very well, the crow was still in the room. Then Mr. McPherrin carefully squeezed out of the classroom door trying not to let the bird out into the hallway. After all, it would be bad to have that naughty bird flying around the entire school! He ran directly downstairs to his office and called the Police Department.

ell, when the Police get an emergency call from a school involving an animal, they call in all of their support systems: the Fire Department, Animal Control and anyone they think might be of help. The Police even called the Brookfield Zoo's Aviary Department to get advice.

NNNNNNNNNNNRRRRRRRRRRRRRRRRRRRRRRRRR

into the school playground came the hook and ladder

truck, the bucket truck, and Police cars with

everyone carrying nets. They were going to

capture this crow if it meant evacuating all the students and

closing down the school!

Four firemen came rushing into the classroom through the window carrying their giant white nets hoping to capture the scary bird. By then the children were all huddled in one corner protected by Ms. Davis with her arms jutting out her sides like ...a dutiful crossing guard.

**L**enore was trying not to laugh because she knew the crow

meant no harm. But with all this confusion even she had to say,

"This is out of hand, they're going to hurt Syd!"

The children watched in amazement as a fireman with net in

hand was being raised up to the second floor in the bucket ladder to capture the

bad bird if it flew out the window. Inside, another firemen chased Syd around the room

trying to catch him. Lenore started yelling, "Don't hurt him! Please don't hurt him!"

Syd looked at the situation and must have thought, "I'm outta here!"

At first he flew in circles to confuse the nets that were bumping into each other

trying to catch him. Then he saw an opening in the window away from the fire

ladders. Syd scooted out that window as fast as he could and flew home to his nest

to escape the mayhem he created at the school.

The emergency was over after Syd fled the scene. The firemen took their ladders down and left the school premises. Mr. McPherrin said, "Close those windows even if you feel like you're roasting! Of course, he didn't mean that. He was just upset and feeling a little silly because the crow had out-smarted them all. Mr. McPherrin got on the PA system to announce to the children and teachers that the crow problem was solved and things were now under control. But, he advised, "Everyone needs to be on 'Crow Patrol' and report any more unusual encounters with a big black crow." Mr. McPherrin didn't understand that Syd meant no harm. As Principal, it was his number one job to keep the children safe…which he did. The school bell rang and everyone went home to tell their parents about their exciting day: how a wild crow had disrupted their lessons and caused an emergency visit from the Police and Fire Departments!

e think Syd learned his lesson too. He never went back to Roosevelt Elementary after that fiasco because it was now getting cold and the windows were tightly closed. Syd had problems of his own: he had to find a nice warm place for a winter home. As the days got shorter, the family could see Syd flying around the back yard carrying things in his beak. It was a small twig that still had some leaves on it or a beakful of dried grass left over from the summer lawn clippings. Lenore worried, "What will happen to Syd this winter? Can we bring him in?"

ne evening while it was still slightly light outside, the family went into the large dining room that overlooked the side yard. The largest room in the house, it had a bay window with a stained glass panel of orange and green tulips at the top. Lenore saw Syd going in and out of the old blue spruce tree that pressed right up against the window. When the wind blew really hard the tree would hit the side of the house with a subtle thump…thumping noise…as it hugged the house for protection.

enore and Jason decided that Syd must have been building a warmer winter nest in that tree so he could watch the family having dinner parties, playing the piano, singing and dancing, and decorating the Christmas tree.

hat was exactly what Syd was doing. Some nights it would snow and the temperature would drop down to a frigid ten degrees below zero. On those nights, Lenore and Jason didn't want to go to sleep because they worried Syd would die in the cold and the wind. But that big old blue spruce made the perfect winter home for Syd.

ven though Syd never came inside our home, he certainly seemed like an important part of our family. Some days he would still come to the corner kitchen window so he could see the family activities from the different rooms in the house.

hen, just as the horse chestnut tree was blooming again in spring, we looked in Syd's empty nest and saw lots of shiny objects he had saved. But we didn't see him. Later we checked out a book on crows and thought that Syd must have found a mate. And as straight as the crow flies, he flew off to make a new life for himself. Maybe he was delighting a new family with his sparkling personality. We don't know why he left... but we never saw him again.

yd had flown away and out of our lives as suddenly and mysteriously as he first came to us. We were so grateful that this magnificent crow had allowed us into his world. He left Lenore and Jason with wonderful memories of a remarkable bird and a true story they can now tell *their* children.

Expanding the Learning -- After Syd, The Crow©™

Syd, The Crow ©™ is based on a true story and is intertwined with interesting sidebars that can be explored further by parents, teachers and the readers themselves.

Here are some special jumping off points for further learning and exploration that can enhance the story experience and become opportunities to expand the study of amazing crows, research the crow's influence on literature and music, explore the Polish heritage and culture, connect weather patterns to Native American Indian folklore, review construction techniques that use well - established water conservation systems, be inspired by the nature of magnificent trees and shrubbery of the Midwest, and discuss the ethics of personal integrity presented by unlocked milk boxes full of cash and easily stolen – but are kept safe in a neighborhood where families respected each other's property, protected the kids and helped one another.

Build a curriculum around these rich concepts:

Yin and Yang: balancing negative and positive (see acknowledgements)

Page #1....the arrow of time…daily home milk delivery...an honor system

Page #3....old-fashioned cistern....'being green'...vegetable garden

Page #5....territorial

Page #7....clarinet, saxophone, violins, piano

Page #8....Polish Christmas Carols, Kolendy

Page #9....house-walk...solid oak antique dining table...grandfather's clock with beveled-edge glass panes…doing chores for an allowance

Page #11…horse-chestnut tree

Page #12…landmark

Page #13…forsythia…iridescent colors

Page #15...blue spruce

Page #16...shiny objects...Opera: *The Thieving Magpie*

Page #17…a murder of crows

Page #19…protective big sister

Page #21…too vs two vs to

Page #23…playing with humans…vs non-humans…and animals

Page #25…homing pigeon…intelligence...dive-bombing

Page #27…Injun Summer…Indian Summer…Cautantowwit…(see footnote)
[1] Stillman, Janice., et al. (2012). Glossary of Almanac Oddities. *The Old Farmer's Almanac*, 220. 136-137.

Page #31…zoo's aviary department

Page #34…hook and ladder

Page #35…mayhem

Page #36…PA System…public address system

Page #37…bay window…stained glass panel…blue spruce

Page #39…tell *their* children about...generational renewal/rebirth/oral history